Ikhda, by Ikhda

AUTHOR'S NOTE

This collection of poetry is intended to free the prejudices of every reader. It was born and compiled with the themes of love, life and whatever – spontaneous emotions are behind it. I believe that poetry is the angel that saves me from heavy scepticism in the life drama. Poetry can be humble, honest, undeniable, and friendly. But it can also be wild, angry, aggressive, and not easily absorbed. It really doesn't matter that we know poetry isn't a conclusion, but a process for tolerating any incident. Life's incidents.

Poetry is a healing drug, or meditation. These poems are not just anti-cliché, but zen and anti-zen. They are a recapitulation of the many human responses to everything that happens in society. My deep adoration of multiculturalism can be read in some of poems which mention space, proximity, and zone.

Happy reading!

Ikhda Ayuning Maharsi
March 2014

Also from the Emma Press:

The Emma Press Anthology of Mildly Erotic Verse
A Poetic Primer for Love and Seduction: Naso was my Tutor
The Emma Press Anthology of Motherhood
The Emma Press Anthology of Fatherhood (May 2014)

The Emma Press Picks:

The Flower and the Plough, by Rachel Piercey
The Emmores, by Richard O'Brien
The Held and the Lost, by Kristen Roberts
Captain Love and the Five Joaquins, by John Clegg (May 2014)

Pamphlets:

Raspberries for the Ferry, by Andrew Wynn Owen
The Dead Snail Diaries, by Jamie McGarry (Apr 2014)

Ikhda, by Ikhda

by Ikhda Ayuning Maharsi

THE EMMA PRESS

Vincent, thank you for showing me the different skies.
Corentin, son, you are inside my blood cells.
Mama, thank you for the wings.
Papa, just don't stop dancing.

'Humanism' in fact, could be defined by its penchant for waste, that is, human waste.
– from *History of Shit,* by Dominique Laporte

THE EMMA PRESS

First published in Great Britain in 2014
by the Emma Press Ltd

Poems copyright © Ikhda Ayuning Maharsi 2014
Introduction copyright © Rachel Piercey 2014

All rights reserved.

The right of Ikhda Ayuning Maharsi to be identified as the author of this work has been asserted by her in accordance with the Copyright, Designs and Patents Act 1988.

ISBN 978-0-9574596-6-3

A CIP catalogue record of this book
is available from the British Library.

Printed and bound in Great Britain
by Letterworks Ltd, Reading.

theemmapress.com
editor@theemmapress.com

Introduction

In the first poem of the pamphlet, Ikhda describes 'the space of absurdity/ a familiar place' where the female protagonist collects 'one hundred flowers'. This is a fitting introduction to the playful, brightly-coloured and seductive world of Ikhda's poems, where her frank enjoyment of the surreal is not a device but an all-suffusing, triumphant worldview.

The poems celebrate the body, particularly the female body, and she exuberantly invokes its animal functions: the 'you' of 'Anatomy' is exhorted to 'pump my breast/ for your kid' and 'drink my spit'; in 'Lys', the speaker tells us 'I have had intercourse so many times with my past', and in the end her sensual pleasures ensure a kind of immortality.

Other people are deftly and humanely conjured. The emotional man walking the roads in 'Atlas in Ubud' is both an eccentric stranger and 'a man that deserved to be desired/ a man that deserved to be loved'. Ikhda looks critically and poignantly at the way humans create problems for themselves – she tells her son, in a painful paradox, 'I hope you don't have the courage to hurt anyone' – but she is always generous with it.

She also isn't afraid of happiness. Her characters do often give themselves a hard time, and she conjures all the weirdness and cruelty of love and lust, but what she really celebrates is connection, for 'what on Earth happens without friction?'.

Alongside these big universal themes, the poems are bursting with flavours, and peppered lushly with Italian and French. Ikhda glories in language, and where it doesn't exist to express her thoughts, she makes it new – witness the gorgeous invented phrase 'gili gili'.

The title of the pamphlet rightly rejoices in Ikhda's unique voice. It's rich, warm and heady. Turn the page, dive in, and find the world lit just that bit more brightly.

Rachel Piercey
March 2014

Contents

Autostrada — 1

Animal — 2

Anatomy — 3

After Work — 4

Anecdote: Paris, Humming, etc — 6

Arguments — 8

Lys — 9

Pinkie Minimus — 10

Gili Gili — 11

Abandoned Melodrama — 12

Atmosphere — 13

Afterbirth — 14

Appetit — 15

Atlas in Ubud — 16

Amnesia — 17

Astrology — 18

Ancient Victoria — 19

Autobiography — 20

Alive — 21

Analogy — 22

Fair enough — 23

*

Acknowledgments — 25

About the poet — 26

Autostrada

Volare
and talk to me about the scars
of the young lady
who is often caught cheating
in her own happiness
then cries for days
walks for kilometres on San Gregorio Armeno street
eating *gelato al pistacchio*
planting basil, flowers, and cherry tomatoes
crying, laughing
cooking, dancing
dubious
jealous
precious
and humming
etc
collecting one hundred flowers
in the space of absurdity
a familiar place
that she calls *amare*
like bees buzzing
o mio amore, quanto distante siamo
and *bzed zzz zed ddd d*
then she keeps running in place
while the people out there are speeding with their cars
on the big *autostrada*.

Animal

I smelled your distinctive
typical smell
from hundreds of kilometres,
branches of trees swaying gently.
I walked along silently
looking for a stud
to marry me once
and feed my *ren* for years.
I don't know if they named me llama
or horse
or dog
or Persian cat
or rabbit
bunny rabbit
and I am not sure
if I am a hermaphrodite
or a female
domestic one
I am a domestic animal female.

Anatomy

Access my brain
shoot lava inside it
put some water into it
lick my bone
change the white into grey
count my heartbeat
say: *I love you, I do, I love you,* and *I do*
for every second it beeps.

Adore my body shape
pump my breast
for your kid
bring chaos to my blood
and whatever –
do whatever.
Colour my hairs
stomp my feet
drink my spit.
I give you access
total access
for using my body.

After Work

You know the definition of the word 'awareness'
a humble-bloomy word about giving expression
and a huge attachment
of love, empathy, humanity
to the target
market

You know how to use emotion
and describe it, cut it off, in a good implementation
fulfilled with amazing visualisation, tagline, body-copy
You know how to attract
human desire
You know how to play on emotions
You know how to make the target feel interested
then consume
You know
you know that all

You know how to increase the response
orbiting the new longing
packed in brilliant story telling
while in the keynote presentation
I always failed in writing
a love letter
for my brilliant co-worker
I believe that you will never know
that the target was me
the target
of your affection

I roar
scream out
stomach ache
and all the little sufferings

I can't handle anymore
until someone is yelling, someone in the market:
O hey, you!
It was her
your loyal client
consumer
that loved you at the very first presentation
and for the very first time
she knew that this project, her love's project
would never be realised
and she hated the after work
the time when you were both parted.

Anecdote: Paris, Humming, etc

Panthéon to Jardin du Luxemburg
We are dreamers
stuck between the giant's feet
the west, the before
We are the past, moving so fast

Rue quincampoix
Look! It's art! No *fond*! No rules! Accepting!
In a little white house
I have found a nice vintage jacket
plus a fancy *grandmére*

Boulevard de Clichy
I am waiting for you
in the corner of justice
epicentrum of west
wind blowing
heartbeating
je suis comme je suis, tu m'aimes?

St Michel, Notre Dame
I have the right to kiss you
passionately grab your sweet body
and after give you a cheap, secondhand book
poetry book
I am a student
life's student

Boulevard de Clignancourt
Lemons
Some of them are crying
While many people are yelling: "Five euros!
Allez! Bien! Bien! Venez vous!"
My Maroc friend needs a good playlist

Opéra
My name is Melodie
the childish young girl from the old town
I like Chinese noodles but I won't make any extra sound

Les Marais to Rue de Temple
No gender
No battle
No victim
We all love to chew and swallow delicious falafel
see the free parking sign
get a tattoo
and walk in the crowds

Trocadéro
Hear the voice of wind
Step on the floor of tomorrow's destination
Where Latin is the starter
And Atlantic is the story teller

Arguments

A man with papers in his hands
was standing near a big oak tree
He was watching the environment in the coffee shop
from the clear glass in front of his face
from the outside
He said to himself: "Should I go there?
Should I sit down beside her
and talk about my dream, my premonition?
Or should I shut up and stay here?"
Then his eyes continued watching
the situation in the coffee shop

There was a fat man looking at the right side
where a beautiful girl was crying,
her finger pointing to a man with a brown coat –
who tried to catch his falling hat
and looked at him (the man outside the coffee shop)
then yelled at him: "What are you looking at!
Go away! Be gone, spotter!"
A man outside the coffee shop became panicked
He yelled: "Watch yourself! She is too pretty to be hurt!
Too young to be torn! Watch yourself –
she is the most adorable female in my life!"

Unfortunately, the room was soundproof
So nobody could hear his voice
They just saw a shaking body out there
and a mouth that tasted madness
then the man with the brown coat sat back with the girl
They were holding hands
back in the honeyed hypocrisy.

Lys

Don't tell me about my roots
or my life before this
Don't tell me about my unopened buds

I was born before you
so much older than you
but still I keep my colour
that you called pain eraser
that I called monument of the ripped

Something that you named maidenhead
for me it is virginity
for me it is the boring lacuna –
what on Earth happens without friction?

I have had intercourse so many times with my past
I remember on Sunday morning
big snails and slugs were vined on my buds
satisfying themselves
with pleasure that resonated
They ate my corps
one by one
slowly
ended
Mmh
Mmh
Mmh
I end
but my roots, not.

Pinkie Minimus

I asked you to keep the promise
using your, my, Pinkie Minimus
like when we were children.

I hoped that you would keep your promise
that we made by Pinkie Minimus
like when we were moppets.

But what did you do
but suck my Pinkie Minimus,
wrestled with worms and germs.

Yes o yes o
my Pinkie Minimus
has been sucked,
licked by your blunt tongue.
O no o no no
what I asked was the promise
of lost childhood,
two Pinkie Minimus
linked to each other.

Yes o yes o
we should have put our wedding rings
on the tiny
platoon
Pinkie Minimus.

Gili Gili

Fight me
and gili gili

Spit on me
and gili gili

Yell above my head
and gili gili

Blend me
and gili gili

As no-one has ever known
how the stringed things
can be perfectly tasted

Gili gili me
Gili gili you

May God
bless every human movement
as your
as mine
as ours
stays
in colours

Let's laugh
like we have enjoyed our last
gili gili

Abandoned Melodrama

You are the fuscous,
and I am the sunblind

You are the light,
and I am the retina

Atmosphere

Like when we spent our time in the south of Jakarta
in a small gallery,
or a place where theatre and poetry are always welcome
or like when I saw your exhibition
in a contemporary gallery in Paris
You never change
for me
Still the same odour
Still the same male instinct
Still marvellous

The photographs
    and phone calls to me from you
        and all the postcards you filled with your sketches
and scratches
Still the same odour
Still the same male instinct
And I have good news for you:

I still have the same tongue
to lick our liquors
You: my dearest proletarian

Afterbirth

In the morning market
early morning market
a beautiful Turkish girl was surprising everyone.
She felt so angry
and her body was trembling.
"Excuse me, sir! Can you pay me more?"
she yelled at the man with the black hat, green jacket,
who was trying to escape from her,
pretending not to listen to anything that she said

"Excuse me, sir! I am talking to you!
You have to pay me more: five euros fifty cents, sir!"
And before the man with the black hat, green jacket
had completely disappeared
she yelled at him:
"I am not selling spoiled meats to you, sir!
This is my meat, my body, you can eat it now, fresh!
I am not selling bad meat, sir! Look at me!
This is fresh meat! Excuse me, sir!"

And all the shoppers in the market
were surprised and speechless;
they watched the breasts, the head,
the legs, shoulder, and the backside of a beautiful girl,
the meat seller, who was really really angry:
"Just give me back my five euros – I – I – just want
my five euros, excuse me, sir."

Appetit

Bon appetit!
and eat your decaying heart
that was wounded in the last flesh orgasm
Bon appetit!
and eat your fingers that are shaking with anger
Bon appetit!
and do your plan to stab your father from behind
then eat his delicious body

or simply change your plans:

Bon appetit!
and forget all soreness without asking for anything in return
Bon appetit!
from me, the injured fly
that is flying over your beautiful vintage plates.

Atlas in Ubud

He was walking on the road of Ubud
wearing the tee-shirt 'Obey the Giant' and smiling
to the old man who had offered him a cigar
He was walking on the road of Ubud
listening to the Balinese *gamelan* music
and trying to erase all the old, dark memories
He was walking on the road of Ubud
selling his big big paintings
to all his web visitors from the origin *Nederlands*
He was walking on the road of Ubud
and praying
and crying
remembering
about his lover
that had been lost and eaten by the waves

He was walking on the road of Ubud
and nodding
He was a man who was walking on the road of Ubud
a man that deserved to be desired
a man that deserved to be loved.

Amnesia

Solea
A girl from Salvador
She never blames her serotonin cells
which deliver all the fake sentiments
She is marrying the one man that she loves, forever
She thinks that the body is a pagan
a place where love and desire dwell
that her place is in the kitchen
where her friends are the kitchensets
Solea, a girl from Salvador
She always forgets the names of the moons of Saturn:
Prometheus, Pandora, Janus, Mimas, Hyperion, Phoebe
She is as illogical as a lottery
and she always feels blessed
as euphoria
She is as detectable as a card game: *Uno*
as lovable as jasmine
as cheap as a lighter
She is Solea
my wife that only has nine brassieres
and eleven underpants
in her cupboard.

Astrology

A linguist and fake astronaut
were talking to each other
about the past, the future.
They were praying together to their god named Liberta.
They were touching each other's postures
and laughing so loud.

The fake astronaut said: "I must have overslept
in the jumbo aeroplane yesterday."
The linguist answered: "It's total logic for me,
my conscious has been woken up
because of your supervision."
And they were kissing each other,
completing their old style possessions.

Ancient Victoria

Kill me Victoria
with your delicious Italian menu.
Before now, your descendants were living inside the trulli
drinking black instant coffee
and reading yesterday's newspapers.
Your breasts are the true sources
of those left behind and running in place
and you are the slave of elegancy that dies in a vacuum
between Latin and future.

Autobiography

A geographical formation
Tension between land and sea
He seemed to dance in harmony with nature
He seemed to drain meaning from spontaneity
moving his fingers slowly
unshod
stepping on white sand
while she was cooking rice in the kitchen

Life is a dance governance
where the shock is normal
and I remember when I was a child
I even asked him: Why are you a dancer?
He answered me: Because we can only celebrate life by dancing.

Alive

Yé Yé Sama nyima
(Elephant is beautiful)
Sama touré nyima
(Elephant is beautiful)
And don't forget to see the skies
Even though they are grey
Let the air clean your body
Let the water wash your indignity
Ohé Djembé fola
(Ohé, playing the djembé)
And please be alive, son, be alive
Diamanté, diamanté, diamala
(Say hello to everyone)
Be alive son, please, be alive!

Analogy

My son
my superlative love
I hope the cells in your body
can mingle well with all the things around you
I hope your thinking
is not limited by east, west, northwest,
southwest, south, and north
Hopefully the differences
always inspire you
Hopefully you will have time to set your feet on the mountain
at the bottom of the sea
or in the air
I hope you don't have the courage to hurt anyone
I hope you ravenously devour your food
grow up well
and smart
My son,
the world is not as warm and funny as your mother's womb
but you are universal walker
and the earth is your playground.

Fair enough

She is enough
of waiting
playing
flying
sobering
singing

For her
        all is fair enough
of meeting
avoiding
limiting

For her
        all is fair enough
        of wanting

She is
        the little bird
eating a tuna sandwich with me.

Acknowledgments

The epigraph on p. iv is from Dominique Laporte's *Histoire de la merde* (Christian Bourgois Editeur, 1978), as translated by Nadia Benabid and Rodolphe el-Khoury in *History of Shit* (MIT Press, 2000).

'Anecdote: Paris, Humming, etc' was first performed in Cité internationale universitaire de Paris in 2011.

'Pinkie Minimus' was first published in *The Emma Press Anthology of Mildly Erotic Verse* (Emma Press, 2013).

'Atlas in Ubud' – all my adoration to the Indonesian poet Sapardi Djoko Damono for his poem 'I want':

I want to love you simply, in signs not expressed: clouds to the rain which make them evanescent.

'Amnesia' was enriched by a flash online search on Wikipedia on the subject 'the Moons of Saturn'.

'Ancient Victoria' was inspired by *Histoire de la merde,* by Dominique Laporte (Christian Bourgois Editeur, 1978), and *Une brève histoire de l'avenir,* by Jacques Attali (Fayard, 2006).

'Analogy' and 'Alive' are dedicated to my little man, Corentin Danau Degoul, and inspired by *Mes Comptines d'Afrique* by Gaëlle Duhazé (Éditions Milan, 2010) and *When the Sidewalk Ends* by Shel Silverstein (Harper and Row Publishers, 1974).

Thank you from the heart to the Emma Press, a hearty – passionate – awesome publisher that has great potential to bring colours to the world of poetry. I would like to say thank you to the lovely Emma Wright for her wonderful cover illustration, and her courage and incredible talent for understanding my wordplays. Thank you to adorable Rachel Piercey for her English editing, thank you for her sensitivity in capturing every stanza and expression in these poems, for her sharp-*bref* introduction.

Thank you to the team of fun-comfortable reading places: the Prince's Trust Tomorrow's Store, the Poetry Café in London and the Albion Beatnik Bookstore in Oxford.

Last, I would like to say thank you to all my life's gurus. All of you. All the brave and angelic personalities I have met in my life. I can't mention you one by one. I hope you enjoy it, folks! :)

About the poet

Ikhda Ayuning Maharsi performed her poetry for the first time in 2011 at Cité Internationale Universitaire de Paris. Her poems have been published in *The Emma Press Anthology of Mildly Erotic Verse* and *The Emma Press Anthology of Motherhood*. She lives in Naples, where she is enjoying her new role as mother to her little boy Corentin.

The Emma Press

small press, big dreams

The Emma Press is an independent publisher dedicated to producing books which are sweet, funny and beautiful. It was founded in 2012 in Winnersh, UK, by Emma Wright and the first Emma Press book, *The Flower and the Plough* by Rachel Piercey, was published in January 2013.

Our current publishing programme includes a mixture of themed poetry anthologies and single-author pamphlets, with an ongoing engagement with the works of the Roman poet Ovid. We publish poems and books which excite us, and we are often on the lookout for new writing.

Visit our website and sign up to the Emma Press newsletter to hear about all upcoming calls for submissions as well as our events and publications. You can also purchase our other titles and poetry-related stationery in our online shop.

http://theemmapress.com

Also from the Emma Press:

The Emma Press Anthology Motherhood
ISBN: 978 0 9574596 7 0 / PRICE: £10

Love and devotion sit alongside exhaustion and doubt in this profoundly moving collection of poems about mothers and the state of motherhood, with poems from Kathryn Maris, Catherine Smith, Ikhda Ayuning Maharsi and Clare Pollard.

Raspberries for the Ferry
BY: Andrew Wynn Owen / ISBN: 978 0 9574596 5 6 / PRICE: £6.50

A stunning debut pamphlet of gorgeous, tart, juicy poems grounded in the past and bubbling with modern verve. Andrew Wynn Owen embraces a variety of formal structures and imbues everything with rhythm, wit and a lively sensuality.

The Held and the Lost
BY: Kristen Roberts / ISBN: 978 0 9574596 8 7 / PRICE: £5

Emerging Australian poet Kristen Roberts sketches sympathetic portraits of characters and relationships against the backdrop of swaying eucalypts, roses and occasional rain. These are love poems with their eyes open and scars defiantly on display.

The Emmores
BY: Richard O'Brien / ISBN: 978 0 9574596 4 9 / PRICE: £5

Richard O'Brien deploys every trick in the love poet's book in this fascinating pamphlet, written in response to a new long-distance relationship. An irresistible mix of tender odes, introspective sonnets, exuberant free verse and anthems of sexual persuasion.
